FOR BUILDING STRONG FAITH

Kenneth Hagin Jr.

Chapter 1
SIX WAYS TO BUILD STRONG FAITH

And there sat a certain man at Lystra, impotent in his feet, being a cripple from his mother's womb, who never had walked:

The same heard Paul speak: who steadfastly beholding him, and perceiving that he had faith to be healed,

Said with a loud voice, Stand upright on thy feet. And he leaped and walked.

— Acts 14:8-10

Many earnest Christians are asking the question: "How can I build a strong faith?"

These people realize that the things they need from God — healing, prosperity, and other blessings — do not come simply because they have been born again. These blessings come through faith.

They realize that faith is not just an act of the will of man; faith is acting on God's Word.

But many do not know how to secure faith for the things they need from God. In this lesson, I will give you a formula to build strong faith for whatever you need from God.

The faith I'm talking about does not come from an act of the will. You can *will* it all you want — you can try to make it happen all you want — but it's not going to work that way. It's not built that way. It doesn't come that way. It comes from the following formula:

First: Surround yourself with that which produces faith.

Every born-again Christian has received "the" measure of faith mentioned in Romans 12:3. Not "a" measure of faith; "the" measure of faith.

ROMANS 12:3
**3 For I say, through the grace given unto me,
to every man that is among you, not to think
of himself more highly than he ought to
think; but to think soberly, according as GOD
HATH DEALT TO EVERY MAN THE MEA-
SURE OF FAITH.**

What you do with your measure of faith
after salvation is up to you — but what you
do with it determines whether or not you
grow in faith.

It's strange to me how many Christians
surround themselves with things that cause
them to be weak in faith. They sit in a church
that does not teach the Word, listening to
somebody tell them it's not God's will to heal,
that it's God's will for us to be poor, and so
forth. They try to stay spiritually alive in
that negative atmosphere where people do
not believe in the supernatural power of God.

God's Word says, ". . . *without faith it is
impossible to please him . . .*" (Heb. 11:6). We
must realize that if we are going to nurture
our faith — if we're going to build it into
something that will produce results for us —
we must surround ourselves with successful

people of God, not negative people. And we must feed our minds and spirits on material that will build faith, not destroy it.

We don't feed faith by reading a steady diet of secular magazines, or viewing a steady diet of secular television.

Turn off that television. Punch the start button of your tape recorder. Surround yourself with things of God; things that will nurture your faith. Listen to people strong in faith — any of the great teachers today. (Just be sure they are teaching you in line with God's Word.)

I'm not saying there's anything wrong with watching television. I've got one in my home. I watch it. Bless God, if I haven't anything else to do — if I'm prayed up, if I don't have to go preach anywhere — and the Dallas Cowboys are playing, I'm going to be watching them!

Another one of my pastimes is reading western stories. I have found one author in particular I read after. Over the years, I have read dozens of his books and they are just good western writing — no bad situations or language at all. I don't do a lot of this kind of reading, but I do a little of it, because I enjoy it. I enjoy life. God expects us to have some leisure and to enjoy our leisure time, but we've got to put God and the things of God first.

I'm not talking about getting out of balance. A lot of people are so far over in some religious areas that they are out of balance with life. Then the devil can get them off on tangents and into wrong doctrine.

The faith walk is balanced. Jesus grew in *all* areas of life — emotional, physical, spiritual, and social. We also need to learn to have God in all areas of our lives, to become well-balanced people.

If you want to have strong faith, surround yourself with the things of faith. Don't live in the negative.

Some, however, live in the negative all the time. If you were to phone them and ask, "How are things going today?" they probably would reply:

"Oh, I tell you, this is the worst day I've ever seen! I can hardly walk for the corn on my foot hurting so bad. And I know the weathers going to change, because that old knee of mine is giving me a fit. The dog got run over yesterday, and rabbits got into my garden last night and ate up everything. Joe called from work a while ago, and he almost cut his finger off. Got it caught in the machine."

How are you going to keep the supernatural power of God flowing in your life if you're surrounded by people who have a form of godliness but no supernatural power? Or those who are opposed to it? This kind of situation will drain you like a battery, because nothing is being put into your spirit to charge it up.

You won't be able to get yourself "started," much less help somebody else out of their troubles.

Let me share a little secret with you: The disciples didn't start their ministry with impressive faith. They were astonished at the things Christ did. When they tried their wings, they didn't do too well.

The disciples had walked with Jesus, they were surrounded by that faith atmosphere for the few short years of His earthly ministry. They had been with Jesus when He calmed the storm, and they had marvelled, saying, "... *What manner of man is this ...?*" (Mark 4:41).

They had seen faith in action as Jesus spoke something and it happened. They had lived in Jesus' atmosphere of victory and faith. They had been filled with the Holy Spirit on the day of Pentecost.

In Acts 4, we see the disciples again. The same Pharisees, scribes, and chief priests who had known them as weak disciples of Jesus looked at them now and realized that they had been — where? Down at the synagogue? No. Down at the Temple? No.

ACTS 4:13
13 ... when they saw the boldness of Peter and John, and perceived that they were unlearned and ignorant men, they marvelled; and they took knowledge of them, that THEY HAD BEEN WITH JESUS.

What did they see? They saw "unlearned and ignorant men" doing the same things Jesus had done. They saw the same miracles being performed. They saw the same atmosphere surrounding Peter, John, and the others that had surrounded Jesus Christ.

They witnessed the same words and the same power. And they knew that these simple men did not receive it any other way except from being in the atmosphere where teaching and miracles were taking place.

It had become part of their innermost beings. Now when the disciples went out to minister it was the same as Jesus ministering!

You and I live in an age where people should be taking notice that *we* have been with Jesus! He was the *Living* Word to those disciples in the first century. He is the *written* Word to us, the disciples of today.

Do you want to work for God? Do you want to move for God? Fellowship with people who believe like you do; people who teach faith. Surround yourself with the Word of God, and that which produces strong faith.

Chapter 2
EXPERIENCE DOESN'T COUNT

Second: Build on the Word of God, not experience.

As I was praying for someone in a service once, a woman came running up, exclaiming, "Oh, I had that same thing! Let me tell them about my experience. It will probably help them!"

I said, "No, I don't want you to tell them your experience."

Why? Because God doesn't always move the same way all the time. Too many people have Him locked in a little box, and they believe God only moves in the confines of that box. If He doesn't move just exactly the way they think He should, they don't believe it is of God. But you can't lock God and the power of the Holy Spirit in a box!

Don't try to make people receive salvation, the baptism of the Holy Spirit, or healing the way you feel it should be received, or the way you have experienced it.

I've known people who received the baptism in the Holy Spirit while seated in a circle with other people. Then they think that everybody must receive just like they did — sitting in that chair in that circle! Now it can happen that way, but it doesn't *have* to. Sitting in a chair in a circle of people doesn't have a thing to do with receiving the Holy Spirit.

Other people have said to me, "Brother, I've dealt with demons, and let me tell you my experience — the way I dealt with them. If you'll deal with them like I do, you'll have more success at casting out demons."

But, no, that's not necessarily true. The *Word of God* tells me how to deal with demons. I'm not interested in hearing somebody's experiences of how he dealt with the devil. God may deal with me differently about handling a certain situation, or I can handle it according to the Word of God.

And while I'm on the subject, I'm going to say something that some people may not like: Everybody who gets rid of a devil doesn't have to throw up. Nor does every person who gets saved have to be delivered from devils.

Most people who are hollering about being *delivered* don't know the first thing about Bible deliverance. They're doing things that I've never found in the Word of God.

I've found only one place in Scripture where Jesus talked to the devils, and He only talked to them then because they started talking to Him first. Every other time He met up with them, He just said, "Come out!"

I've never found in the Word that it took Jesus three weeks, two days, and thirty minutes of calling them out by name, either. When He said, "Come out!" they came out. Deliverance is not a long and painstaking process.

People talk about having all these devils and how long it took for their deliverance. If they had had all the devils they claim they had, they would be raving mad. Most persons are not devil-possessed. If a person is possessed, you can't control him, and he has to be put in an institution.

But there are a lot of people whom the devil is oppressing. There is a difference, "

Every devil in hell is scared of the Name of Jesus. Jesus has already defeated them, so you do not need to come against them with anything but His Name. All you've got to do is know who you are in Jesus, speak the Word, and the devil's got to go. It doesn't take three weeks. You'll understand that if you study what the Bible has to say about this subject.

I was reading an article on healing the other day in a major Bible commentary. It was written by a man who has a string of titles behind his name. Do you know what he had the audacity to say?

"If it had not been for Dr. Luke's traveling with Paul [the Apostle Luke was a physician], and having his medicine kit with them on that island where they ministered to the chief, they would have been in trouble."

I never saw that in Luke's writings. In addition to the Gospel of Luke, Luke wrote the Acts of the Apostles. Therefore, he himself wrote the account of their shipwreck on Melita (Acts 28) and the account of the healing of the crippled man at Lystra (Acts 14). I don't see anywhere in Acts where Luke said, "I gave him a physical examination, found thus-and-so, and treated him in this way."

Do you want to get spiritual? Do you want to get in on the move of God? Do you want to get faith? Then build on God's Word. Notice that Jesus didn't build on experience. He taught the Word. When He defeated Satan, He kept saying, "It is written . . . it is written . . . it is written."

Chapter 3
GOD HAS NO SECOND BEST

Third: Look to the Word of God, not someone's personality.

If you're going to have strong faith to receive from God, build it on the Word; not someone's personality.

Did you ever watch Brother Hagin preach? He doesn't put too much of his personality into it. He keeps his personality suppressed so people will look at what the Word says.

The Bible says, *"He sent his word, and healed them, and delivered them from their destructions"* (Ps. 107:20). He didn't send a personality. He sent His Word. Forget about personalities.

Many people come to Tulsa, Oklahoma, and say, "We came down here for Brother Hagin to pray for us."

Sometimes we have to tell them, "He's not in town," or "He has shut himself away for a time of prayer, fasting, and study." We add, "Someone else will be glad to minister healing to you. We've got all our RHEMA instructors here. We've got all kinds of personnel. Any one of them could lay hands on you and pray for you."

"No," they say. "We want Brother Hagin. We don't want *second best*."

I tell them, "There is no second best with God. It does not have to be a certain man laying hands on you for you to be healed."

"That's all right," they say. "I'll just go on over to Oral Roberts!"

Then, if someone tells them Brother Roberts is not in town, they say, "Well, I'll just go to Kenneth Copeland. *He'll* pray for me."

You see, people begin looking to personalities instead of the Word of God. But a person is not going to heal them. It's the Word of God that's going to heal them. And the Word of God says — speaking of any believer, ". . . *they shall lay hands on the sick, and they shall recover*" (Mark 16:18).

That means a little child could lay hands on you and pray for your healing. And if you would believe like God's Word says, you could be healed from a child's prayers just as easily as you would from an adult's or a preacher's prayers. The Bible does not even require "someone who is anointed" to pray for healing; it says "*. . . them that believe . . .*" (Mark 16:17). *If you're a believer, you qualify to lay hands on the sick!*

When people come to me and say, "My faith is weak, and I need healing," I suggest they go through the Word of God and memorize all the Scriptures concerning healing.

They say, "Well, that will take a lot of time."

I reply, "You'll find that Brother Hagin already has put those Scriptures together in a minibook called *God's Medicine.* Get that book out every time you think of it in the next two weeks, and begin to quote those Scriptures out loud. Read them until they become a part of your innermost being. Build the Word inside you."

I have seen those same people later, and they've said, "Do you know what? I did not even have to go forward to be prayed for! I just started walking in the light of the Word of God, and my sickness disappeared instantly." You see, the Word can do it.

God has given us many different ways to

receive healing from Him. One is through prayer by the laying on of hands. Another is by the prayer of agreement. But the highest and most rewarding way is to receive in line with God's Word. Walking in perfect harmony and unity with God — just you and God — is the highest kind of faith.

But, thank God, God has promised other means for those of us who sometimes don't attain to the highest kind of faith. So don't put down the person who does not have strong faith like you do.

If you have to, go down to this brother's level of faith and agree with him on that level. Find out what he can believe for. Then begin to put the Word of God into him so you can lift him up to your level of faith.

You yourself need to know what the Word of God says so that when symptoms, financial peril, or disaster strikes, you can compete in the arena of faith.

If you know what God's Word says, every time Satan starts to take a swing at you, you can say, "It is written . . ." and block it. When he comes at you with another weapon, you can say, "It is written . . ." and that same

shield of faith is lifted, blocking all of the
enemy's darts.

Chapter 4
THE REWARDS OF OBEDIENCE

*Fourth: Obedience is necessary to
build strong faith.*

1 JOHN 3:22
**22 And whatsoever we ask, we receive of him,
because WE KEEP HIS COMMANDMENTS,
AND DO THOSE THINGS THAT ARE PLEAS-
ING IN HIS SIGHT.**

JOHN 15:7
**7 If ye abide in me, and my words abide in
you, ye shall ask what ye will, and it shall be
done unto you.**

Notice the connection between these
Scriptures. In First John, the apostle wrote,
". . . *whatsoever we ask, we receive of him,
BECAUSE we keep his commandments . . .*"
We cannot keep His commandments, however, unless we know what the Word of God
says — unless His Word abides in us.

John also said, *"Beloved, if our heart condemn us not, then have we confidence toward
God"* (1 John 3:21).

How are we confident? We are confident
if our hearts don't condemn us. We have confidence toward God that He will do exactly
what He has said.

Obedience.

God does not require us to walk in the
light of some archangel. God does not require
us to walk in the light of some man's doctrine. God does not require us to walk in the
light of church tradition. God does not require
us to walk in the light of a denomination.

God *does* require us to walk in the light
of the eternal Word of God. That's what we're
required to be obedient to.

When we walk in the light of this Word,
then we can have confidence and know that
what God said He will perform, He will do;
then we have the right to claim what is ours.

If we do not do what is right in the sight
of God and do not live the way we should,
there is no way we can have confidence that
God is going to give us what He said we could
have.

He can't.

I don't care how much He wants to —and He wants to minister to every one of us — He cannot give it to us, because He cannot condone the way we're living. Giving it to us would imply that His stamp of approval is on what we are doing, and it cannot be.

Many people are going around making faith confessions that are never going to come true. These confessions are never going to come true because the people are not living in line with God's Word.

There is a right way to live in line with God's Word, and it doesn't have to do with a set of rules — dos and don'ts — either. It is obedience to the Word of God. Obedience to the Spirit.

Then we have the right to claim what is ours as children of God.

Chapter 5
IF YOU'RE PROUD; YOU'RE PROUD

Fifth: You must have humility.

A lot of people are *proud* of their humility!

I've met a lot of people across the country who are bragging that they are "faith people." Their attitude is, "If you're not where *we're* at, you haven't got it, brother."

As far as I'm concerned, this is a sectarian point of view. It is not biblical.

The disciples got into this same attitude in Luke 9. They got prideful and puffed up. When a child was brought to them they couldn't cast the tough, stubborn, unclean spirit out of him (v. 40).

Jesus explained to the disciples that this kind comes out only by prayer and fasting.

They lacked humility and discipline. This hindered their faith.

The disciples had not been able to understand Christ's conversation regarding His imminent death on the Cross. They were looking for the Kingdom of God to be set up on earth then and there. And as we read further in Luke, we see other reasons why the disciples could not perform this great miracle.

They began to discuss their own importance (v. 46). They began to argue over who was going to sit where in the coming kingdom! They even asked the Lord about it:

"Can I sit here, Lord?" They were building themselves up. "Look who we are! We're somebody!"

They even began to talk about who was *greatest* in the kingdom! Notice their spiritual poverty in the following verses:

LUKE 9:49,50
49 And John answered and said, Master, we saw one casting out devils in thy name; and we forbad him, because he followeth not with us.
50 And Jesus said unto him, Forbid him not: for he that is not against us is for us.

So we see a sectarian spirit rising among the disciples. "Hey — you're not with us!" they said. "You quit that! You're not part of our little group." But Jesus said, ". . . *Forbid him not: for he that is not against us is for us*" (Luke 9:50).

Notice something else. Immediately after this, we find the disciples accompanying Jesus into a town that would receive neither Him nor His message.

When James and John saw this, they were furious. They asked hopefully,

". . . Lord, wilt thou that we command fire to come down from heaven, and consume them, even as Elias did?" (Luke 9:54).

Jesus immediately rebuked this kind of spirit. He told the disciples, *". . . the Son of man is not come to destroy men's lives, but to save them"* (Luke 9:56).

Some people have thought they have a monopoly on the gifts of God. The devil has used this kind of thinking to destroy, divide, and split apart the real move of the power of God.

We need to be humble before God — but I'm not talking about being a doormat. I'm talking about realizing that we would not be where we are today without the grace and love of God.

Sometimes we preachers get the idea that if people aren't ministered to under our ministry, they aren't going to get helped. But sometimes it's laypeople, not ministers, who promote this idea. Laypeople can be partly responsible for ministers' getting lifted up in pride when they have favorite ministers and won't allow anybody else but their favorites to pray for them or minister to them.

So you see, if we're not careful, we lift up other people to where they think they're somebody. We believers *are* somebody with the power of God — but we're *nothing* without it.

Saying we are children of God is vastly different from sticking your thumbs under your lapels and boasting, "Bless God, I'm a man of *faith* and *power*! If you're not believing God — if you're having to take any medicine or go to any doctor — you're sinning!"

The man who says that is a liar. Yes, there is a better way than going to a doctor and taking medicine, but you're not sinning if you do these things.

I want to tell you something — if you don't have enough faith to be healed, I'll get you to a doctor and get you some medicine to keep you alive long enough for me to sit down with you and pump you full of the Word of God so you can walk away *healed*!

How many more people would be free today if someone hadn't stood on their soapbox and said, "Hey, don't have anything to do with those people over there, because they

24

don't wear our denominational hat."

How many more people would be in the kingdom of God today if the Pentecostals had not been so hard on those who just didn't understand the infilling of the Holy Spirit. (*Both* groups believed in salvation through the blood of the Lord Jesus Christ!)

You're going to see people in Heaven, and you're going to wonder how they got there, because they didn't come out of *your* mold. But there's only one mold they must come out of. They must know Jesus Christ as their personal Savior, and they've got to live a godly kind of life — according to the Word of God.

Yes, I believe everyone should go on to that next step and get the infilling of the Holy Spirit and all God has for them — but if they accept Jesus Christ and live a godly life, they're just as saved as you or I, praise God.

Let's get away from our sectarian thinking. We need to have some humility. We all live down here on this earth together.

I guarantee you, if we live in line with God's Word, we can build a faith that can bring part of heaven down here while we're going to heaven.

I'll tell you why: All that is in heaven belongs to us — all of it is ours — because we have become heirs of the promise.

There is no monopoly on the power of God. One group does not have it monopolized. I can tell you what group *does* have it monopolized — however the group of the blood-bought, born-again Church of the Lord Jesus Christ.

I'm not talking about *a* church — I'm talking about *the* Church, called in Greek the *ecclesia*; the called-out ones.

Chapter 6
'HEY, DEVIL! I'M TALKING TO YOU!'

Sixth: To build strong faith, you must have holy boldness.

This is something many people need badly. Most people are afraid of the devil. They would like to hide from him.

But you're going to have to be able to boldly claim what belongs to you in the Name of El Shaddai, the God who is more than enough.

You're going to have to be willing to stand, look the devil square in the eye, and say, "You hoodwinked me and fooled me for the last time! Either get out of the way, or get ready to get run over!"

Bless God, I'm not afraid to face the devil. In fact, if I see him about 50 yards down the street, I call, "Hey! Hey! Devil! I'm talking to *you!*" He ducks around a corner. He doesn't want any part of me.

He doesn't want any part of an individual who knows who he is in Jesus Christ, because Jesus defeated Satan. He knows that you are going to start speaking that Word with your mouth. And every time those words come out of your mouth, it's like somebody hitting him with a whip. So he doesn't want any part of you.

Yet the Church has been so beaten down — so cowed — that its members are not bold anymore. Instead of going out *looking* for the devil, they hide if they see him coming. I really believe some people have more reverence for the devil than they have for God. When they start talking about the devil, they get *quiet.*

Brother Hagin tells about being in California in 1950 in the middle of a flu epidemic. Everything was shut down. Some preachers were standing around talking with the pastor after church.

They said, "Do you think you're going to have to shut this meeting down?"

The pastor replied, "No, Brother Hagin won't let me shut it down."

One of the preachers said, "Well, aren't you afraid you'll all get the flu? Man, you're down to almost nothing. There were hardly fifty people here tonight. I had an evangelist over at my church. He closed the meeting down to go home and get ready to have the flu. Said he felt it coming on."

About that time, my dad walked up.

They said, "Brother Hagin, aren't you afraid you're going to have the flu?" (They said it *quietly*.)

"No," he said. "I'll tell you something. I'm not ever going to have the flu."

"Oh, Brother Hagin!" one man whispered. "I wouldn't say that if I were you! The *devil* will hear you!"

Dad just reared back and said loudly,

"Yes, that's the very dude I *want* to hear me!

"I want him to know that I know who I am in Christ Jesus; that I know what I have because of what Jesus has done for me; and that he's not fooling with some novice who doesn't know what he is doing.

"I *want* him to know he's not going to run over me.

"I want him to know it now, so I don't have to have a fight later on."

You've got to have holy boldness. You've got to be willing to be in the forefront of the battle.

Young people at a church I once co-pastored used to say, "Ken, you pray funny."

I would ask, "What do you mean?"

They said, "When you pray, it's just like you were talking to your daddy."

I said, "I am. I'm talking to my Heavenly Father."

I don't have to crawl to Him on my hands and knees and beg and plead any more than I have to crawl into my dad's office in Tulsa and beg and plead with him.

I walk in there boldly. If his door is shut, I knock, open it, and walk in. Why? Because that's my father. I'm his son. I have the privilege of being in there. You think about that!

When my daughter, Denise, was little and visited our offices, it didn't matter to her if my office door was closed. She would come popping through that door. That was her Daddy's office!

She would also go bouncing through every closed door into her Pa-Pa's office. There could be ten people sitting in his office, but she would go straight to her grandfather and climb up on his knee. Why? Because that was her right and privilege. She was part of the family, an heir of the family.

I want to tell you something: We are joint-heirs with Jesus Christ. We have a right to be bold about our position. We must learn to walk in that position. We must learn to walk in that boldness — even *when you're hurting* — proclaiming God's Word.

Boldly take hold of whatever you need from God. Boldly proclaim it. Grab hold of it with the tenacity of a bulldog that will grab hold of a bone and won't turn it loose.

I grabbed hold of this Word many years ago. I'll never relinquish my hold on the

Word of God. I'll walk through life victorious because this possibility faith belongs to me. I'm going to walk in the light of God's Word, quote God's Word, and be what I'm supposed to be in the Kingdom of God. And you can, too, if you want to.

Boldly, authoritatively proclaim your deliverance in the areas of finance, healing, habits, or whatever. It is the words spoken by your mouth that is the creative force. It is your mouth that will turn loose the power of God for you as you quote God's Word.

Boldly begin to proclaim what is yours according to the Word of God. Think of a Scripture that covers your particular situation. Stand on that Scripture. Boldly proclaim and quote that Scripture.

If you need finances, boldly command the ministering spirits (angels) to cause finances to come to you. Boldly say (and say it loudly), "Devil, take your hands off of my finances! You have no authority and no right."

If you need deliverance from a habit, begin to command that you are free according to the Word of God, because "greater is He that is in you, than he that is in the world" (1

John 4:4). The Greater One already has
delivered you and set you free. Right now you
are going on record that you already have
been delivered and you're proclaiming that
deliverance now. Be bold. Put your voice to it.

We had a little black poodle for many
years. Pierre was our first "child," because we
got him right after we were married. He trav-
eled in the ministry with Lynette and me in
those early days.

I could say, "No, Pierre," and sometimes
he would pay attention to me, and sometimes
he wouldn't. But when I turned around and
said, "No!" that dog would stop in his tracks.

What made the difference? The authority
and the way I spoke to him. That is the way
you have to deal with the devil. As long as
we're mealy-mouthed, he's going to keep
hanging around, doing what he's been doing.

But if you open your mouth and speak
with authority — backed by the Word of God
— he's going to turn and run, because the
Word of God says, ". . . *Resist the devil, and
he will flee from you*" (James 4:7).
Get what belongs to you!

CONFESSION:
It is done.
It is done.
It is done.
Because the Word says it,
I will not be moved by what I feel;
I will not be moved by what I see.
I will only be moved by what God's Word says.
I will only speak what God's Word says.
I am delivered.
I am free in Jesus Christ.